Weird America!

AMERICA'S ODDEST FADS

By M.H. Seeley

Gareth Stevens
PUBLISHING

Please visit our website, www.garethstevens.com. For a free color catalog of all our high-quality books, call toll free 1-800-542-2595 or fax 1-877-542-2596.

Cataloging-in-Publication Data

Names: Seeley, M. H.
Title: America's oddest fads / M. H. Seeley.
Description: New York : Gareth Stevens Publishing, 2017. | Series: Weird America | Includes index.
Identifiers: ISBN 9781482457476 (pbk.) | ISBN 9781482457490 (library bound) | ISBN 9781482457483 (6 pack)
Subjects: LCSH: Popular culture–United States–Juvenile literature. | Fads–Social aspects–United States–Juvenile literature.
Classification: LCC E169.12 S4535 2017 | DDC 306.0973–dc23

First Edition

Published in 2017 by
Gareth Stevens Publishing
111 East 14th Street, Suite 349
New York, NY 10003

Designer: Sarah Liddell
Editor: Ryan Nagelhout

Photo credits: Cover, p. 1 (arrow) Mascha Tace/Shutterstock.com; cover, pp. 1, 29 (trolls) Joe Schilling/Getty Images; sidebar used throughout zayats-and-zayats/Shutterstock.com; brick background texture used throughout multipear/Shutterstock.com; screen texture used throughout donatas1205/Shutterstock.com; pp. 4, 5 Adam Cuerden/Wikimedia Commons; p. 7 Rklawton/Wikimedia Commons; p. 9 BILL BRIDGES/Getty Images; pp. 11, 15 Bettmann/Contributor/Bettman/Getty Images; p. 13 Everett Historical/Shutterstock.com; p. 14 Vangert/Shutterstock.com; p. 16 LoriLee/Wikimedia Commons; p. 17 Bill Johnson/Contributor/Denver Post/Getty Images; p. 18 Keepsmiling4u/Shutterstock.com; p. 19 Alexandrabush5/Wikimedia Commons; p. 20 Dario Sabljak/Shutterstock.com; p. 21 Senator2029/Wikimedia Commons; p. 23 Rick Madonik/Contributor/Toronto Star/Getty Images; p. 24 Al Freni/Contributor/The LIFE Images Collection/Getty Images; p. 25 Charla Jones/Contributor/Toronto Star/Getty Images; p. 26 chippix/Shutterstock.com; p. 27 Allan Grant/Contributor/The LIFE Images Collection/Getty Images; p. 29 (frames) Sabelskaya/Shutterstock.com; p. 29 (tie-dye) Michael Warwick/Shutterstock.com; p. 29 (bell bottoms) Flickr upload bot/Wikimedia Commons; p. 29 (Barbie) James Leynse/Contributor/Corbis Historical/Getty Images; p. 29 (go-go boots) SteinsplitterBot/Wikimedia Commons; p. 29 (lava lamp) Paket/Shutterstock.com.

Printed in the United States of America

CPSIA compliance information: Batch #CW17GS: For further information contact Gareth Stevens, New York, New York at 1-800-542-2595.

CONTENTS

Words in the glossary appear in **bold** type the first time they are used in the text.

PANORAMA DRAMA

Have you ever seen a dance move or toy on TV and then started to see it everywhere? Some people may even become **obsessed** with it, but usually just for a couple of months. Then, everyone just moves on to something new.

That's called a fad, and one of the very first American fads was **panoramic** pictures! Wandering artists would go from town to town selling hand-drawn panoramas to a town's citizens. These artists would first map the town by walking the streets, then imagine what it looked like from an elevated viewpoint high above the town streets. Panoramas were just the start of the many weird and wonderful fads that have captured America's imagination over the years.

This 1902 print was based on a drawing by Thaddeus Mortimer Fowler, one of the most famous panorama artists of his day.

Stop the Presses!

No artist could hand-draw 250 images overnight. Panoramas were made using lithography, a printing process where printmakers draw on a block of limestone, moisten the limestone with water, then apply ink. The ink sticks only to the lines of the drawing. Paper is laid on top and pressure is applied to transfer the ink from the stone to paper. Artists sold the pictures in bulk: the smallest amount a city could buy was 250 prints!

panorama of New York City

RACCOONS ON YOUR WHERE?

It gets cold out on the **frontier**, as the Europeans who were just starting to **immigrate** to America discovered. These settlers stole elements of dress and **culture** from Native Americans already living there. One of those was the "coonskin" hat: an entire raccoon pelt (fur), head and tail included, was made into a hat to keep the ears and head warm.

In the 1950s, Davy Crockett—a popular TV character based on a real-life frontiersman—made the hat a popular fashion statement among American boys and girls. The hats were so popular that a candidate for president— Estes Kefauver—even wore one to get more votes!

Beg, Borrow, or Steal

Many fads become popular when, like the coonskin hat, they're adopted from another culture. This is called "cultural **appropriation**," which happens when an outside group takes something (such as a style of dress) from another group and claims it as their own, often against the wishes of the creators. The original meaning and importance of the thing are often lost.

Raccoon-skin hats were a Native American invention. Europeans adopted the style as they moved further into the harsh frontier.

I'M STUFFED!

Telephone-booth stuffing was a fad that had many lives. In 1959, 25 students in South Africa packed themselves into a phone booth to set a world record. In response, college students across the United States began trying to fit more in.

The craze was so extreme that people lost weight to make themselves smaller. Groups even began to accuse one another of cheating! No one, however, ever beat the South African record. Though the "telephone-booth stuffing" craze had mostly died out by 1960, it came back to life later in the form of "car stuffing."

One for the Record Books

Guinness World Records is a book that has all kinds of crazy records in it. Did you know that Pizza Hut recently set a record for highest pizza delivery—to the top of Mount Kilimanjaro, which is more than 19,000 feet (5,791 m) tall! The tallest house of cards measures 14 feet 6 inches (4.4 m). Can you break that record?

The "stuffing" fad didn't end with telephone booths and cars. People also tried to fit themselves into hollow trees, trains, and even outhouses!

CALLING THE DEAD

Ghosts were everywhere during the **Victorian** age in America. At least people thought they were! The 1800s were a period of many scientific breakthroughs, but they were also a time when many people believed that ghosts and spirits were not only real, but also available for conversation.

During these years, a popular activity was the séance, which is when a group of people try to contact spirits of the dead to ask them questions. Séances were conducted by mediums, people who claimed they could see and talk to the dead. But most people think séances were just tricks.

Houdini's Medium Myth-Busting Squad

Even though Harry Houdini made his living performing magic tricks and escape acts, he believed mediums were criminals who wanted to trick people into giving them money. So he put together a team of detectives who went from town to town proving that local mediums were lying when they said they could talk to the dead!

The Fox sisters were America's first mediums. They claimed to own a haunted table that helped them talk to the dead.

DANCE THE NIGHT AWAY

Have you ever danced so long your feet started to hurt? Well, if you could dance all day, you could have won some money for it in the early 1900s!

The only rule of a dance marathon was "don't stop moving." People had to dance for 24 hours a day, with only short breaks for sleeping every hour or 2. These marathons would go on as long as there were couples still standing. The longest one, held from August 1930 to April 1931 in Chicago, Illinois, lasted for 5,148 hours and 28.5 minutes and included a cash prize of $2,000!

Dance for Your Dinner

During the Great Depression (1929–1939), when many lost their jobs and their money, dance marathons were a way to earn cash and free food. Eventually, people began to worry that so much dancing and so little sleep could be bad for the body, and many towns decided to ban dance marathons.

These days, many schools and other groups use dance marathons to raise money for charity.

THIS TASTES FISHY

In 1939, a fishy new food craze took over college campuses across the United States: goldfish gulping! After a Boston newspaper featured a story about a Harvard student swallowing a live goldfish, students at colleges across the country competed to see who could swallow the most fish at one time.

Some people added salt and pepper or drank milk to help with the terrible taste. One swallower ate mashed potatoes to get rid of the taste! But most people swallowed the goldfish without chewing. The eventual winner of the "Goldfish Swallowing Derby" may have been Clark University student Joseph Deliberato, who swallowed 89.

Wanna Bet?

This odd fad started because of a $10 bet! Harvard freshman Lothrop Withington Jr. bragged to his friends that he had once eaten a live fish, and they bet him he wouldn't do it again. A reporter was there to see him swallow the bet-winning goldfish, and the goldfish-gulping games began.

Open wide! Lothrop Withington Jr. said he practiced for days by eating baby goldfish and tadpoles in order to win the bet.

SIT! STAY! SEW!

What makes a cute skirt cuter? A dog! In the 1950s, you couldn't go outside without seeing a teenage girl in a bright pink skirt with a poodle stitched onto it. These skirts gained popularity both because of their fun look and because of how easy they were for anybody to make at home. All you had to do was cut out a large circle and add an **appliqué**!

No two poodle skirts were exactly the same, and many skirts had whole stories told by pictures on them. The original poodle skirt was **designed** by Juli Lynne Charlot, who kept the design simple because she couldn't sew.

Poodle skirt designs quickly took on a life of their own because they were so easy to make at home.

Sock Hop

One place you were sure to see many poodle skirts was a sock hop! These high school dances were so named because everybody had to remove their shoes and dance in their socks. Lots of famous dance fads gained popularity at sock hops, such as the jitterbug, the stroll, and the handjive.

HAIR TODAY, GONE TOMORROW

Before the days of exchanging phone numbers or e-mail addresses, young men showed their interest in young women by asking them for a hairpin as a **keepsake**. But in the 1880s, this sweet **tradition** took on a strange new twist: theft! In this odd game, young men would secretly steal young women's hairpins or collect them if they fell out.

The idea was to collect more hairpins than anyone else and display these very small trophies in scrapbooks and albums. Each pin was labeled with a description of the young woman and the date the young man "earned" the hairpin.

Hairpins might be one of fashion's oldest tools—they're believed to date back to prehistoric times!

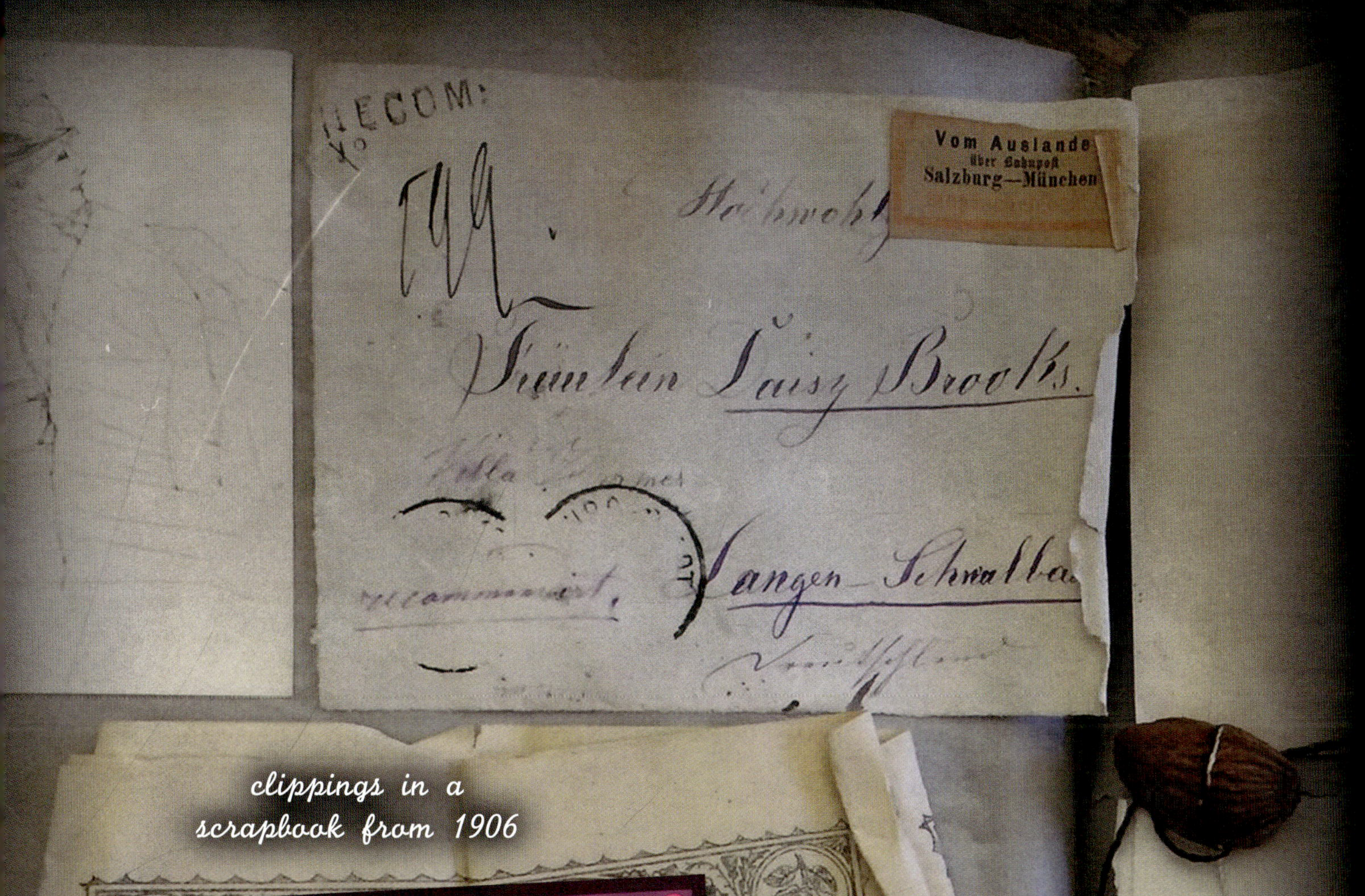

clippings in a scrapbook from 1906

Scrapbooks

Scrapbooking is no fad: Though they first **documented** life in the 19th century, their earlier forms date back to the 15th century! Originally, scrapbooks usually held things like letters, poems, newspaper clippings, recipes, and class schedules. Eventually, they began to include photos and other modern inventions. Today, many scrapbooks are entirely digital.

TURN, TURN, TURN

Another weird dating fad popular in the late 1800s was called ring turning. This strange game was supposed to help a woman find someone to marry. When meeting a man wearing a ring, a young woman would turn the ring two or three times.

After she had turned rings about 24 times, she had to find a married person (either man or woman) and turn *their* wedding band twice. After *that*, the next man she shook hands with was said to be her future husband! The process, however, took so much time that it was actually banned from some workplaces.

White Weddings

The white wedding dress is often the first thing that comes to mind when thinking about weddings. But brides used to wear all sorts of colors when they walked down the aisle—even red! American brides began wearing white after Queen Victoria of England made it popular overseas.

It's impossible to
know where the strange "ring
turning" fad came from.

WRIGHT'S WRONG

In 1943, a General Electric engineer named James Wright was trying to make synthetic, or man-made, rubber in a lab. He mixed two chemicals, boric acid and silicone oil. The mix didn't make rubber, but he did make a sticky goo still popular with children today: Silly Putty!

It wasn't called that until 1949 when a man named Peter Hodgson saw the substance at Ruth Fallgatter's toy store. Hodgson bought $150 worth of the substance and sold it in plastic eggs. By the time Silly Putty was shown on the *Howdy Doody Show*, it was a must-have toy for kids.

Copy, Stretch, and Bounce

Silly Putty was and still is popular because it can do odd things most solids and liquids can't do. The putty can bounce, stretch, and stick to walls. It can even copy ink from newspapers when it's pressed against the page! The images and writing can then be stretched to make funny faces and shapes!

Hodgson made millions of dollars selling the sticky stuff. But Earl Warrick, another man who invented Silly Putty while working for Dow Corning, only got $1 for his patent!

PET ROCK

Could a rock be the perfect pet? Gary Ross Dahl, inventor of the Pet Rock, seemed to think so. Rocks aren't noisy, they don't need to be walked or cleaned up after, and you'll never have to pay for food or to take them to the vet.

A booklet titled "The Care and Training of Your Pet Rock" explained that the Pet Rock's best trick was playing dead. It appeared on television shows and even had its own theme song: "I'm in Love with My Pet Rock" by Al Bolt! Though this fad began as a bit of a joke, it appealed to young and old across America.

The Pet Rock came in a box that had air holes cut into it—so the rock could breathe, of course.

Tamagotchis

Two decades after the Pet Rock craze swept America, another pet took its place: the Tamagotchi! This digital chicken-like alien was a pocket-sized toy that allowed its owners to hatch an egg and care for their alien by pressing buttons to feed, care for, and clean up after it.

ATOP A FLAGPOLE

Like goldfish gulping and telephone-booth stuffing, the flagpole-sitting fad kicked off because everyone wanted to be the best. Alvin "Shipwreck" Kelly, a professional **stunt** performer in Hollywood in the 1920s, was dared to sit on top of a flagpole for as long as he could—and "as long as he could" turned out to be 13 hours and 13 minutes.

Soon huge groups of people gathered to watch flagpole sitting. After others broke his 13-hour record, Kelly decided he wanted to regain his flagpole throne and reset the record by remaining on his perch for 49 days!

Stay Awake!

Flagpole sitting required a lot of balance and concentration. Kelly once stayed on a flagpole even through a harsh storm. He even shaved and bathed up there! In Baltimore, Maryland, a "Keep Kelly Awake Club" formed to come at night and make lots of noise to keep him from falling asleep—and falling off the pole!

This couple loved flagpole sitting so much they celebrated their wedding atop a flagpole!

THE SWINGING SIXTIES

A decade is a period of 10 years, and no decade in the United States was more famous for fads than the 1960s. New dances like the Twist and toys like Barbie dolls and lava lamps became big hits.

The 1960s may be most known for its fad fashions. Long, wide-legged jeans called bell-bottoms were very popular. Many people made their own tie-dye shirts. These were shirts dyed many colors in a swirled pattern. Women in the 1960s also wore low-heeled boots called go-go boots. Some fashion fads even come back in style—bell-bottoms were popular again in the 1970s and 1990s, and some people still wear tie-dye today!

Hippies

Many young people in the 1960s were called hippies! They used "hip" words like "far out" and "groovy" to talk about things they liked. They wanted peace, listened to "trippy" music, and wore many of the fad fashions of the time like bell-bottoms and tie-dye.

GROOVY '60s FADS

go-go boots

tie-dye

troll dolls

lava lamps

bell-bottoms

Barbie dolls

GLOSSARY

appliqué: a cutout fastened to a larger piece of material

appropriation: the act of taking without permission

culture: the beliefs, practices, and religions of a group of people

design: to create the pattern or shape of something. Also, the pattern or shape itself.

document: to record, as with photos, printed accounts, and written notes

frontier: land that has not yet been fully explored or settled

immigrate: to move permanently into one country from another

keepsake: something kept in order to remember a person or event

obsess: to occupy the mind completely

panoramic: having to do with a picture with a wide view

stunt: an unusual or hard feat requiring strength or skill

tradition: the handing down of information, beliefs, and customs of one generation to another

Victorian: having to do with popular taste during the reign of Queen Victoria of England (1837–1901)

FOR MORE INFORMATION

BOOKS

Bix, Cynthia Overbeck. *Fad Mania! A History of American Crazes.* Minneapolis, MN: Twenty-First Century Books, 2015.

Lindop, Edmund, with Margaret J. Goldstein. *America in the 1920s.* Minneapolis, MN: Twenty-First Century Books, 2010.

Niven, Felicia Lowenstein. *Fabulous Fashions of the 1950s.* Berkeley Heights, NJ: Enslow Publishers, 2012.

WEBSITES

Bad Fads Museum
badfads.com
Visit this site to find more funny fads throughout US history.

Crazy Fads
crazyfads.com
This site lists lots of fads from the 1920s all the way to 2010—some of which you might recognize!

INDEX